CASHMERE DIARIES

'Silken weaves of enchanting amorous verses'

Conceptualized & Edited
by
Gitanjali Kapoor

First published in 2020 by

Becomeshakespeare.com

One Point Six Technologies Pvt Ltd.

119-123, 1st Floor, Building J2, B - Wing, WadalaTruck Terminal, Wadala East, Mumbai, Maharashtra, India, 400022.T:+91 8080226699

WORDIT ART FUND

This book has been partially funded by the Wordit Art Fund
Wordit Art Fund helps deserving authors publish
their work by providing monetary support
To apply for funding, please visit us at
www.BecomeShakespeare.com

ISBN - 978-93-90266-13-5

Come let's drench in 3am conversations of
nothing but love.

Evoking untapped feelings

beneath the canopy of stars

and the moon blushing from above.

CONTENT

<u>Title of the poem</u>   <u>Page no.</u>

Gitanjali Kapoor

Baishali Deb

Japjit Kaur

Reema Ghosh Majumdar

Ritu Sharma

Seema Joglekar

Sujitha Sukumaran

Sumana Chakraborty

Yogita Jadhav

"In silken weaves of gold and red

was she moonlight in daylight

or poetry draped in cashmere thread."

ABOUT THE AUTHOR:

Gitanjali Kapoor, the ideator behind "Cashmere Diaries" is a beautiful single lady in her forties from Mumbai, India.

Known by her pen name Laughing_Soul she's been creating waves in the literary world through her poems which have been featured in various publications in India as well as internationally. She has also invented a poetry form called "Mirror Alphoppbet" which is quite popular amongst writers worldwide.

Author and Publisher of three Anthologies and a solo collection of Poems,"Priceless Pearls" she now explores her sensuous side with "Cashmere Diaries". Being a fire sign her ambrosial Sagittarian Aura reflects in her woven tapestry of words.

Instagram ID: laughing_soul_poetry

NOSTALGIA OF THE FIRST KISS

A thousand times the Sun sets
leaving the horizon blushing
in a hundred hues,
and every night the stars dance bashfully
to the Ocean's flirtatious tunes.

But all it takes
is the petrichor of April showers
to intoxicate my senses
with nostalgia of bygone days of ours.

Now you are lean
and I'm a few folds of withering flowers.
But don't you forget the spring
we first kissed during the Moonlit hours.

You enthral me even today
with your salt and pepper greys,
And drowning in your hazel eyes
is how I love to end my fleeting days.

MONSOON OF ECSTATIC WILDFIRES

Those dark clouds,
that bewitching rain
lure me for a walk with you
down the memory lane.

A little thunder,
a vast storm brews
an umbrella for one
and we were two.

Sparks flared
as brushed arms bare
fingers entwined
arousing the interlocked emotional snare.

T'was a night of sweltering shivers
gasps and moans
and scintillating quivers.

T'was a night we created memories
palpitations high, smokey eyes
the most erotic accessories.

a rainfall t'was of burning desires
a monsoon of ecstatic wildfires
my heart aches for a little thunder
a walk in the rain with feelings asunder.

FLAMING PASSION

You've held me deep,
entangled dark fantasies seeped
and I felt euphoria silently creep.

Like a galaxy of stars
drawn towards a black hole,
you've touched my bare soul.

Flaming meteors I see in your eyes
and as I lay in your arms
an ocean of love surges between our sighs

I bloom a full Moon as you hold me deep
like the Azure night skies,
our senses defies
entangled dark fantasies seep.

PHOTOGRAPH

I flip the pages of the album
things from a distance smile;
I pull out a photograph
and it brings close all those miles.

I dust the dust off the memories
and once again walk down the aisle;
You and me were so unprepared
yet things from a distance smiled.

A mug of coffee, a strong filter
exactly like how you did beguile;
Rain of aromatic nostalgia
and things from a distance smile.

And now it's onset of winter
I have to say goodbye ;
Let's leave the rest for a next time
whilst things from a distance smile...

BOUGAINVILLEA
(Clogyrnach Poetry)

Bougainvillea in my hair
gift by you worth a solitaire.
Winds kiss it softly
as your love haunts me.
Yet fondly, oft I wear.

Sultry breeze caress the buds sore
like a conch I lay washed ashore.
Shriveled blooms of art
hold I close to heart
as we part, evermore!

"Someday when I wouldn't have words for you

That day you will become my words unsaid."

ABOUT THE AUTHOR:

Baishali Deb is an author, a content writer and a blogger. She hails from Karimganj, Assam and is currently pursuing her bachelorette degree. She has been a part of various national and international anthologies along with being a national level yoga competitor and a table tennis player.

She loves listening to music and being a nature lover, she likes to observe things happening around. Holding a certificate in digital marketing, she helps the start ups to set up their website and gain their visibility in digital platform.

You can follow her on instagram @vaishali_deb for regular updates.

SOMEDAY

Someday,
when I wouldn't have words for you
that day, you'll become my words unsaid.

Someday,
when you wouldn't have time for me
that day, I'll become your watch instead.

Someday, when I would feel low
and cuddle up in the bed
that day, you would talk to me
giving me strength and courage.

Someday,
when you would be in a ruffled mood
and wouldn't want to speak
that day, I would become a friend
to your numbness.

Someday, when we would have a fight and
decide never to talk again
that day,
our words would speak to each other
in the engraved silence of time.

THE LAST TIME

The last time we talked,
I was happy being your priority.
The last time we talked,
I smiled throughout the call.
The last time we talked,
you told me
how you spent your whole day.
The last time we talked,
you kept talking and I had nothing to say.

The last time we talked,
I didn't want the call to end.
We laughed together
making fun of each other.
We didn't even see the time
nor did we bother.
The last time we talked,
you asked why I speak so little
And you have so much to say?
The last time we talked
I wondered about the differences we had.

The things,
That we've never talked about.
The last time we talked,
We kept silent for sometime
Not knowing what we should talk about.
The last time we talked,
I wanted it to last forever,
Not knowing if it would ever.
The last time we talked,
I closed my eyes
And made up my mind
That even though unsure
If I'm ever going to see you again,
I promise, when our eyes meet,
I would save your reflection
For the rest of my life.

HOPE

Embroidered with dreams
and some pearly chime
our life surrogated different means.

Beaded with memories
and the effluent reminiscence
the summon of life detached for our sake.

The feeling of agony
and the music of symphony
hoarding the dearth, separating us by miles.

I roam around, round and round
with sanguinity
to be with you, just with a little hope.

YOU

You are the poetry I write about
the melody I sing about
you are the sweetest friend
I've ever come around.
You are the droplet of rain,
on a hot summer day.
The goosebumps I get,
whenever you are near
are enough to tell me
you are everything to me that's dear.

You are the sunshine.
And the rainbow after a shower,
you are my joy and my power.
You are the flower
that blossoms in winter.
The fragrance of petals
that flows around,
you my love are the one
my heart has found.

IF

And, if I was asked
to write something about you?
I would probably write about your smile.
The one that still lingers on my mind.
The curve that squeezes your eyes small,
making you look even cuter,
and my heart enthrall.

And, if I was asked
to write something about you?
I would probably write about your hair,
the one that keeps mischievously falling
on your brow every time you tilt your head
And how you fail to manage it
and how I enjoy watching it.

And, if I was asked
to share a secret about you?
I would probably share about the wishes
that really mean to you
the good lucks that count
and the satisfaction you soul feels
when someone cares for you.

And, if I was asked
about your favourite colour?
I won't hesitate to answer it
'Black and White'
because that's what I believe
would be your answer
the one that you told me years ago
and I still remember
not knowing if it's still your favourite
but I remember.

"My heart fluttered in crazed frenzy

soaked in smoldering passion of your gaze

your drugged breath, a whispering fire

etched kisses on my face."

ABOUT THE AUTHOR:

Japjit Kaur, an English teacher by profession, started writing as a hobby which soon developed into a passion. A rebel at heart and a perfectionist, she has a very positive approach towards life. Her strength is her family and immense faith in divine providence.

She is the editor-in-chief of her school editorial board and has taken part in numerous writing events and won laurels too.

Compassionate and caring by nature she tries her best to contribute in whatever way she can for the betterment of society.

THE ENTICER

You knocked at the door of my heart
with those dark stormy eyes
Curled lips which breath doth part

You enchant me with your breath
tumulting my senses
as you plant butterfly kisses along my neck

You enchant me with your voice
as its huskiness envelops me
soothing, calming, telling me to rejoice

You enchant me with your eyes
as I feel the smoldering passion of your gaze
my senses you paralyze

You enchant me with the smell of you
as we meet in a zephyr of emotions
drowning me in sensations exotic and new

You enchant me with your touch
as your hands explore in angelic symphony
and my hold tightens in a frenzied clutch
yes you enchant me darling

as I soak in the essence of you
I need you to be real, when nothing else is

TRULY! MADLY! DEEPLY!

I am crazily and consummately
in love with you
Every moment bewitching
luscious things I accrue
Your embracing arms
are like heaven
For my traumatic soul
finds peace therein
Your lethal smile disentangles
the chaotic mess I am in
And skilfully silences
the typhoon of thoughts within
I feel so sane and secure
as you make love to my insecurities
You are the calm I seek to assure
while storms rage around in all ferocity

SUMMER ECSTASY

Placid sky, glittering orbs
hand in hand
we amble down the forest trail
swathed in a silvery strand

Summer breeze gently blows
caressing our cheeks
ruffling the hair
and through the branches the moon peeks

Flower laden branches
a canopy, beauteous rare
showering blessings
certainly love is in the air

Magical moments
charmed we move closer
heartbeats prancing wildly
in a warm embrace enfold each other

The fiery trail of cascading kisses
beautiful, deep, enigmatic
like a whiff of euphoria
drench me in ribbons psychedelic

My lips parted on their own accord
souls merged, everything felt so right
A wistfulness came into my eyes
as I transcended into a fanciful flight.

CHARISMATIC LOVE

You entered my life
like a cosmic fantasy
painting my darkness
with magical hues of ecstasy
Destinies conspired for this to chance
I found the one who made my cells dance

I felt the knots untie themselves
things happening deep inside
squelched emotions unknown to myself
now squirmed to breathe freely
Our souls met in a Celtic knot
to embark on an eternal journey of thoughts

I felt my barriers crumbling down
the quagmire of should not, could not
which kept me pinioned to the ground
were blown off like dandelions
The knot of am not which never let me rise
broke, as I soared with my love by my side

LIFE - A WILD LOVE STORY

Life is alluring
a phantasmagorical reverie
Embrace its persona
in all vivacity
It holds within
all that you lusted for
With lips quivering
drink in the celestial liquor
Dig in your nails
hard into the skin
While you face the furor
with uplifted chin
Let the powerful sensations
overwhelm you
Enriching you with the freshness
of morning dew

"Your scent

makes me fall in love

my skin, wears the truth,

it does.."

Cashmere Diaries

ABOUT THE AUTHOR:

Born and brought up in Mumbai, Maharashtra, Jeanette is a part time teacher and a full time Mom who has been in love with writing since she was a little girl.

Not a fan of the fast paced life that is prevalent today, she lives her life in slow motion. A journey that commenced purely from her veins at a tender age of 11 leading up a path of fantasy and amusement. The knowledge of this ownership of a set of her words called poetry created for her a sense of freedom from the harsh reality. She loves that world and now only wishes to touch hearts of her readers and transport them to the 'fairyland' she lives in.

She loves everything connected with art, gardening, cooking, music, drawing, painting, collection of stamps, reading, etc.

This is her first anthology.

I FOUND YOU

When on my most desolate path
that needed not just
sprucing up
but overhauling
not a sprinkler
but an intensive one
gentle and constant

You pruned my thorns
and withered-ness
dug a bit to root out
skeletons and brokenness
strew a big chunk of compost
covering deep depression
gently soothed with salt-less tears
and oh! so constantly

I HAVE TO TELL YOU SOMETHING

My surreal life has held discreetly within
the unhealed wounds of my festered heart.
Concealing it from the universe was futile.
She knew.
Trying her best to comfort me.
Placate my lesions.
Holding scabs from falling off that were
bleeding from sadistic inquisitiveness.
She soothes it with her balmy fondness
for her melancholic child
who you so euphorically
handed your wedding card
to a generation ago.
Today, life has come a full circle
when I saw a broken you with only tears
to fill your empty basket.
I limp my tattered pieces to fit them into
your jig-sawed life
trying to say....
I have something to tell you,
A secret only to you, because the entire
universe already knows it.
And I wonder....
Do I still need to say it?

ONLY YOU

Numerous rivers so refreshing
with that 'come hither' look so inviting
and I will settle for none
but the one you bathe in

My 'land' holds many roads so scenic
that will entice you if you're not quick
but I will travel the one
that leads to you

Myriad species of exotic flowers
that maybe a prospective lover
all I want is the one
that smells of you

The multitudes of mountains
they beckon me to solicit peace
how could I concede
when I know my respite is only in you

OUR RECEPTION

We bled our souls bare by the river
that drove down a lonely path.
I remember how we purposefully chose
this place for 'Our Reception'.
For the grand finale of our turning point,
to move our separate ways.
Greeted by pining trees all misty eyed
showering us with tears.
The mountains
whistled us a parting serenade.
My ears still ring its tune
when I think of you.
Now this picture hangs on my eyelashes
reminding me of the reason it was chosen.
Our story was beautiful
From 'Once upon a time'
To 'The End'.

TOUCH ME LIKE

Touch me like rain touches the earth
when she's hungry.
Tread softly at first creating a carpet
like sprinkle of diamond sweat
on her parched skin.
Let her take her time and soak it all in.
hold on!
she'll want more and at a faster pace.
Give it to her but with a lot of grace.
She'll heave and moan
that's her.....gratitude shown
and don't worry
about being excessive.
She'll lap it up,
hoarding, for the time
when drought sticks around
just in case you'll never be back.

Cashmere Diaries

"Love... the roots of truth felt from the depths of the earth, the purity of two influent rivers flowing into one soul, the faith of the sun rising in the morning.

Love... heaven's most sought- after blessing."

ABOUT THE AUTHOR:

Jeni Ayn Herbert is a poet from Buffalo,
New York and Miami, Florida.
She is a paralegal by occupation, a mother
of four, and a guardian/advocate of children.
Her dreams and interests are in youth
inspiration and she currently owns a
nonprofit organization encouraging youth
internationally.
Jeni Ayn loves to write poetry on love,
suffering and justice.

ESCAPE

I closed my eyes
To feel your lips
Upon mine
One last time
Before you escaped.
Our lips locked in time
Holding onto the blending
Of impulse and fate
A destiny mapped in
Each other's breath taken.
Soul to soul
Inhaling one another's dreams
As if we were exchanging
Promises of eternity
Trusted in each other's
deepest secrets.
The scent of forever
on our naked bodies
The touch of love
In each other's hearts
I could feel you began to drift
An escape into the river of my soul.
Our bodies began
To resemble

The shoreline and the tide
Our reflection became
heaven and earth on a sunset night.
An escape
Into my mind, body and soul.
I kissed you one last time
Before I let go.
Of me.
Because I knew
When I awoke
You would be gone.
Escaped into me.
As I escaped into you.
No longer you and I
As we became lost
In each other's heartbeat.

"Circumlocutions are like northern sun glowing

enough to blaze my blank sheets and

connecting the gaps via nib."

ABOUT THE AUTHOR:

Nirupama Jayaram is a well versed author in the languages of English and Tamil. She had contributed to more than 20 published English and Tamil poem anthologies, in her relatively short writing career of three plus years. She discovered her passion of writing before few years and now venturing it. She is splitting her time between homemaking and awe-inspiring writing.

LOVE-BURN

Loving
Caring
Hugging
Blooming
And then your feel loving caring glee,
Blazing the soul, hugging, blooming me

FLAVOURING FEEL
(HAIKU SONNET)

Love flames in my heart
Yearning for your arrival
Me oblivion

Nurturing your feel
Love blooms spread its aroma
Blushing like dawn sky

My senses twisted
Veins and nerves that are tuning
Oh! I'm seducing

Filling my spaces
Your silhouette traded mine
Stealing my secrets

Sniffing the feel ached heart heals
Flavours of you and me seals.

EPITOME(ZANILA)

Wow to gulp the juice of desire
Started to sense feel of love
The feel made me thrill, I start to quill
In the feel of love soul starts to bow

Douse me with your effervescence love
Let me drink and soak in it
I start to quill the feel made me thrill
Seduced mind started to dance a bit

Felt the warmth when I'm in your arms
Mind relaxed with a gentle sigh
The feel made me thrill, I start to quill
Epitome of love made me fly high

Grabbing you in my heart, felt solace
Art learnt to live for long age
I start to quill the feel made me thrill
I begin to read you page by page

MYSTICAL SAGA
(HAIKU SONNET)

Love sweet as honey
Made me to float on cloud's smoke
Guess it's the rare feel

Subtle feel feels you
Flying like a parakeet
I'm oblivious

Completely blank
It's blatantly my first love
Aching to embrace

Bliss to chant your name
Love profound germane to me
Feel never egress

Came as oeuvre of my life
Adorning my poetic saga.

EPITOME OF LOVE

Beauteous eyes filled with kohl
Longing to see you as a whole
Our love tale has its own whimsical bend
Oh my beau let's travel till the end

Sit on the scintillating chariot come to me
Take me to the Phanerozoic aeon
to feel the glee
My soul is nothing without you
Come! Break my chained up hesitation
by your hue

Douse the desiderate feel of fondness
Allow the aesthetic soul
to break the oddness
Oh! Chinook will you be my postman
Carry my whim and bequeath it to my man!

"The ancient well of solitude
The very echo of your thought
could light up the sky
my feet are entangled
in the quicksand of silence."

ABOUT THE AUTHOR:

Reema Ghosh Majumdar, a poetic heart from childhood, participated in various writing activities till university level. Now in her mid-forties and a mother of two beautiful daughters has started a poetry page "Angelic Verses" on Facebook and have been writing regularly on several creative platforms.

MY MOONBOW

Effervescent moments
Of honey and dew
It was never in my resources
To forget you
Enchanting ecstasy
Covered the Milky Way
I bottled up frivolous fireflies
To lighten up my gray

Ephemeral mortality
Wooed eternity
I blew up my casket beneath the soil
The cool breeze that touches you every night
is the spirit of me

Endearing arrangement
Pact signed with moon
I would come out with her every night to
touch you
And before the sun rises, in her crevices
would return soon.

CARVED AND SEALED

Certain people just dissolve in
Like chimes they hang on your heart side
window
Letting the sunshine in iridescent mode
Synchronously rhythmic
In tones variant
Ushering calm in turbulence
Glorifying triumphs
Walking talking rehabs
Also being partners in crime
Out of blood connections
Enhancing your faith by being the weaver of
your gossamer dreams
Your pounds in body or wallet
Doesn't lure them
They are the keepers of your naked soul....

HEART LOCKER

Treasures.
A thing of value
We love you.
Cherish you
Adore you and keep you under lock and key.
Yes! Underground you are kept,
Far from the roving eyes.
Preserved safely in the deep recess of heart
and mind.
We keep you...
Season after season
Oblivious to your claustrophobia.
Ignorant to your desire
to dangle on the ear with pride.
Or caress the neck with graceful shine.
Perhaps even hold the wrist
with glittering solidarity.
Instead kept aside.
Tarnished with time...
If not limelight,
at least a moonlit night
An appreciative glance or two....
Air and light and oxygen.

Treasures ...
the ones we hurt
Are hurt too if abandoned.
Some says LOVE is a treasure too!

FORBIDDEN

All those prickly words
And the cajoling scars
All those luscious vines
Picked and plucked
Weathered feet on move
Barrel after barrel
Crush splash crush splash
Bloody amber stored
Intoxicated by its own spirit
Mostly in cellars to grow old
And lonely they live bubbling
Gurgling, throughout fermentation
Counting days to be poured in crystal
sparkles holding molten ruby
Gliding through the throat
Which once upon a time sang love songs.

"Eyes did the whole conversation and words were jealous, they had no part to play in their love story."

ABOUT THE AUTHOR:

Ritu Sharma, a Virgo, settled in Bangalore holds a degree in Chemical Engineering but is a Human Resources Practitioner by choice. She plays many roles in a day be it of a doting mom to her kids, a supporting wife, a hobby writer, a homemaker, a caring daughter, a loving sister, a confidant friend or a working professional. Her interests lie in writing, gardening, reading and yoga. She loves to travel and cherish the treasure of pictures that she clicks while exploring new places. She makes her own sunshine by living her dreams every day. She believes strongly in Karma and always tries to bring happiness in others life. She writes under the pen name soulful_ritu and you can find her on Instagram.

A MYSTICAL STORY

Her vivacious soul met
A charismatic spirit,
Exchanged a soul gaze
Igniting strong passion forever,
Eyes enchanted
What heart desired for,
She coyly smiled
As he extended his hand,
She poignantly danced thereafter
Dreaming rest of life in his arms,
An agape love story
Stupendously was crafted,
There was no fault in their stars
'T was just a supernal fairy-tale!

LIFE WITHOUT YOU

One dark night,
I was intensely distressed,
Reflecting on a scary dream,
Which left me in despair,
Abruptly I was awakened,
With feeling of grave loss,
Jolted me austerely,
I kept pondering whole night,
Why my thoughts,
Were so weird and,
Frightening devoid,
Shaken up I felt,
Cried my heart out,
Imagining my life when,
You will be no more,
Sleeping in my arms,
Under this silvery moonlight,
How dreadful would that life be,
Turned and I hugged you tight from behind,
Calmly I slept once again!

LOVE NEVER DIES

You be the winsome candle,
I be the blazing flame,
let our feelings rekindle,
expressing penchant,
for the words left unsaid,
Between you and me!

INK WEDS PAPER

I will be the indelible ink,
You be my revere paper,
Let us inscribe a love story,
Passionate to read,

When paper asked the ink,
'Will you marry me?'
Since then like inseparable souls,
They are entwined,

Forever within me,
Your loving heart shall reside,
World would know finally,
I am yours and you are mine!

LOVE SPEAKS

When his eyes convey zillions of your own
feelings
without a conversation,
When you understand his priorities and
Do not complain,
When his parched eyes crave for your
attention
Yet not wink,
When you see his dreams as yours and hope
They come true in a blink,
When his queer way of wooing you in
crowd
Makes you blush,
When you shy away thinking that your
laughter
Makes his day,
Yes! Love speaks a language but to hear it
You have to immerse in his deep eyes and
feel it for you.

"If passion is a crime

Then I am a prisoner of time

This heart and body of mine

yields each time"

ABOUT THE AUTHOR:

Seema Joglekar, born romantic...happily married for thirty plus years; proud mother to two grown up sons and a lovely daughter in law...true believer of love; of passion; of dreams!

With a never-say-die attitude, she has lived her life never losing sight of the one thing that binds us all…Love.

THE OTHER WOMAN

Tingles down my spine
These shivers divine
Lost in paradise
In the oldest rhythm of time

Is it wrong? To feel so sublime
When I know you are mine
If only for an hour
One night, at a time

To her, you must return
When my hour is done
Every night, each time

I am your woman
She is your wife
She is who the people know
As the inspiration in your life.

No question I ask
For answers there are none
I just lose myself in paradise
Giving in to the oldest rhythm of time.

WOMANHOOD

When you touch me, I can feel the glow
Oh hold me, let love flow.
Your eyes cherish me
Sparking like dark wine
This body of mine gives in each time.

If passion is a crime
Then I am a prisoner of time
This heart and body of mine yields each
time.

Even the petals blush,
On seeing such lust,
The passion in your eyes
Unlocks my desires.

Drunk in your essence
My body undulates like a flower in the rain
Wanting you
Needing you
Time and again.

AIRBRUSH HAPPINESS

Look at our faces
Glowing and tanned
We walked by the sea shore
Laughed in the sand

Immediately it was clicked
Put on display
Without facebook
Would we have laughed this way?

The mountains in the backdrop
The snow on their caps shine
We clicked the margarita glasses and lime
For Instagram each time

The perfect picture we captured
To be put out there
A perfect memory we created
Out of time and space.

These pictures on display
Captured no pain
Don't show no strain
Of our fights and sulky nights
Just our sweet smiling faces

Perfect families on perfect holidays
The perfect loving couple
Even perfect old bodies
Defying gravity
On the time lines these went
Year on year
The perfect life
Defying time and reality

Then, one day, suddenly,
You walked away
And, I sit here alone
I look back at our life
And wonder
For how long did I
Airbrush happiness this way?

"I don't regret being messy the whole day,

but I do about the night

in which I dressed up

and waited for you..."

ABOUT THE AUTHOR:

Sujitha Sukumaran is a 25 years old Computer science post graduate from a farmer's family in Kerala. She started scribbling as 'redpaint' since 2016 as a therapy to deal with the bipolar disorder. She is currently writing on instagram page 'talesbyred'. Apart from writing she loves farming, photography and dogs.

LOVE FEVER

I simply laid near to him,
just to watch him sleeping,
street light pierced through the window glass
to kiss his beautiful face,
and I found it to be shining more today.
I wanted to touch that nose tip,
but I didn't.
There was a smile left on the corner of his
lips and the taste of our last kiss, maybe.
This is how I wanted to end all my days,
by seeing his face, feeling his warmth.
I wanted him to wake up
in the middle of his sleep,
like a baby waking up and making sure that
his mother is there.
So I can cuddle him to sleep again.
My heart was craving to shower soft kisses
on his rosy cheeks and silky forehead,
but my heart refused to wake him,
Slowly the sleep started defying my eyelids.
I don't know when I fell asleep.

I felt something moving on our bed.
I felt something creeping through my hair.
His fingers,

I felt his breath on my neck.
I found his eyes on me,
his arms curled around my waist.
I wrapped him so tight we bloomed in each
other's hands with our love and warmth..
while cuddling him he buried his face on my
chest.
My heart whispered 'mine'.
My eyes walked through the window,
I saw two doves sitting in the sunshade of
our opposite apartment.
I could hear their voice,
They were sharing some romantic tales,
I guess.
While falling asleep again he made a voice
like that dove,
that made a wave in my calm waters.
I felt my baby is in seek of my attention.
I held him closer.

The night was so calm and we were too late.
before closing my eyes I looked at those
doves,
I wish they could see us back.
I wanted them to be jealous.
I don't know why.
I closed my eyes.
Smiled and whispered to me...
This moment is happiness,
this place is heaven and this man is mine!

AMOROUS VERSES

*   You were good at making
mansions for me to visit,
but I was in need of a home to stay.

*   My blood was
the drastic redpaint
in the canvas of love,
clot yet bright.

*   Then I realized
I can give so much of me
to things I will never love,
like I gave my days, weeks,
months and years to this distance
that parted our crossed fingers.

*   For being so deaf
the world gifted me a man
who has music in his eyes.

*   When you left
    I paused myself and acted dead
    its not you who failed me, I am.

*   One day,
    you will come back to
    me in places I waited for you
    but there you will see nothing
    except my bones
    the arrow from your bow.

*   I always managed to conceal
    this love in my veins
    but the wounds you made
    makes it leak often.

*   I am cursed with the bravery
    of expressing my emotions
    to the world which is blessed
    with the cowardice of not feeling it.

* For not expressing the waves
   of emotions
   that crashed against the rock of your
   rejection
   all these pages are filled with
   melancholic tales jotted in tears.

* But darling,
   I felt so loved when you said
   you have no feelings for me
   I saw your eyes
   regretting this rejection
   I saw your lips shivering
   to shower love on mine.

"Sipped coffee in your arms ,

lips conjoined ,

warmth enhanced."

ABOUT THE AUTHOR:

Sumana Chakraborty is an ardent, passionate writer in her mid forties and a mother of two beautiful daughters. She's done her post-graduation in Microbiology and is a teacher by profession. Since her college days she developed a natural inclination towards writing, from then there's no looking back. Myriad colours of life inspired her quill to etch poetries one after another which she captured with the help of her imagination in her pages. Drawing and painting are some of her other favourite activities where she finds solace and contentment.

Instagram ID: sumana.chakraborty.733

SERENADE

Into that variegated delicate resplendency
Sunrise, sunset amalgamated
You and I coalesced to
that bewitching existence
At which the world amused, enthralled
Enkindled we, the symphony of love
To that extent of fulfillment
To that extent of mellifluous serendipity
That blushed the golden western horizon
Flickered the twinkling stars
Moon smiled with shy
Visage of mine like a scarlet bride
With endless thirst sinking
Into the sappy lips of thine.

GLEE

Love that rules your heart
You can hardly hide
But still you blatantly deny.
Hearkening
Incessant symphony inside.
Senses numb,
Logical perceptions
Solemnly sway
Out of sight,
Maddening wilderness
Billowing in utter delight,
Amour's visage twinkling
In your lovestruck eyes.
Coincidentally,
These are the inklings of
Love, smiling behind.

IS THAT LOVE

Love is that hue of life
That lingering pleasure
Which you cherish and admire
which you persistently
Prefer to adhere close
To your dear heart
Gossamer of dreams you weave
Between what said and
what to be said next
Then giggle unknowingly
Trying to realize more than
What it actually is.
Then again start weaving
And spinning new colourful yarn
Of fantasies and illusions
Around hard core reality of life
Relentless humming
who can deter even
amidst million chaotic thunder.

I often get confused
Cannot discriminate
Between love and infatuation
Their nature and culture

Their actual position
In heart, brain or in optic nerve
Age, sex, caste, religion no bar
No spring no winter
Love thy name ...
A sempiternal quest
Akin strong westerly tempest
Perhaps that dearest mayhem
Which uproots, rehabilitates being
Into a new colourful, soothing world
Of inexplicable glamour.

REMINISCENCES

This mind still maddens for him
This mind still walks with him
Far beyond lofty mountains
Into deep tranquil forests
Beyond the farthest horizon
Where we drowned in surreal oblivion.

Those sparkle in his eyes
That serenade during night
Bewildered my mind
My first star in twinkling night
I gave him my heart and mind.

It's now only my silhouette with him
This mind still maddens for him
This mind still walks with him
But now only and only
In this heart's realm
Which bewildered my life.

RENDEZVOUS

Do not utter those
Unsaid words today
I read it long long ago
From your dark eye's sparkle
Utterly smitten.

When lovestruck night's
Symphonic serenade
Used to mesmerize
Half blossomed buds
I laid by your side
And they bloomed vibrantly
Bathed in next morning dew
To tell a tale fresh, fragrant anew.

Don't utter it,
Don't reveal it,
Keep it safe and sacred
In casketed mind's
Secret space.

When time will arrive,
I would pluck it safe
Aromatize it relentless

With my heart's fragrance
Cause love's safest venue
Is that throbbing muscular space
Embrace me with that
When required
By your silent eye's deepest gaze.

"Dreams in her eyes

Sunshine in her heart

A life of wildflowers

Is all that she'd want!"

143 | Yogita Jadhav

ABOUT THE AUTHOR:

Yogita Jadhav belongs to the cultural city of Pune where the company of books is rather inevitable. She possesses a degree in Law and has keen interest in aesthetics. She's serving in the Income tax department for the last 26 years. Her hobbies include drawing and reading. She is a lover of poetry and puts her thoughts to words sometimes. Being an avid reader since childhood, writing became the natural step towards her self expression. She believes in spreading positivity through her words and leaving behind some thoughts to ponder.

IN FLESH AND IN ETHER

Perched on my eyelids
I carry a little dream
Drenching in the thoughts of us together
Greeting the feeling
with a smile and a gleam
Grown fondly in the presence of each other
Now, every moment I believe in carpe diem
We shall live in my dreams,
in flesh and in ether.

SUNFLOWER IN WILD POSIES

You make me feel special every single day
I'm made for the heavens, is what you say
The twinkle in my eye reminds you of afar
But I'm nothing more than that falling star.

You never fail to get me a bouquet of roses
But I'm just that sunflower in wild posies
Never wondered why I'm not that exotic
dish,
Coz I'm just that soulful soup you relish.

For you I've always been the lucky charm,
I'm but that humble cherry on top, sitting
calm
Yet again, beauty lies in your eyes, I trust
Else, I'm pretty much speck of earthly dust.

CAPTIVATING

While I was sizzling in your arms
the whole galaxy's been firing up
Smoldering in your flaming charms
my lusting desire's gearing up
Our gaze fixed in burning inferno
as passion ignites our fiery path
Captivated, you hold me oh so tight
in your embrace oh my amorous knight!

MUSE

Come, make me your muse tonight
Write me a poetry for every star in sight
Walk me down the aisle of moonbeam
Reconnect me to my estranged dream
Sing me the song of eternal love
Shower upon me stardust from above
Take me on a trip of the constellation
Lead me to the way of salvation
And when the sky's about to be sunlit
Embrace me in a farewell, as we split

BLOSSOMING

Since the time I met you
It's only to you I incline
My bud longing to bloom
Facing towards your sunshine

Since the time I met you
I'm glowing in the cheeks
Every petal soaking in your hue
Embracing the fine pinks

Since the time I met you
I'm counting oh so steadfast
"He loves me" "He loves me not"
Still holding onto my petal last

Since the time I met you
All my nectar's getting sweeter
My soul is nothing without you
For darling our love runs deeper.

151 | Yogita Jadhav

DEDICATION

To our parents who taught us to love and dream and drape our feelings in cashmere weaves, we love you!

To the Almighty for gifting us the most wonderful muse, the moon, and the myriad stars, the twilight and the darkness which bedeck our verses. Thank you!

To feelings forlorn and somber verses we're beholden to for they've healed us!

And to those who've loved us with our scars, who entwined their lives with ours, Thank you, in our poetic endeavours we breathe you!

Last but not least heartful gratitude to our quills, the feathers on which our words perch. Thank you!